BUILDING
BEAVERS

by Kathleen Martin-James

⌐ Lerner Publications Company • Minneapolis

Lerner Publications Company
A Division of the Lerner Publishing Group
241 First Avenue North
Minneapolis, MN 55401

Website address: www.lernerbooks.com

Words in *italic type* are explained in a glossary on page 30.

Library of Congress Cataloging-in-Publication Data

Martin-James, Kathleen.
    Building beavers / by Kathleen Martin-James.
      p. cm. — (Pull ahead books)
    Includes index.
    Summary: Introduces the physical characteristics, habits, and natural environment of the North American beaver.
    ISBN 0-8225-3628-5 (hc. : alk. paper). —
    ISBN 0-8225-3632-3 (pbk. : alk. paper)
    1. American beaver—Juvenile literature.
[1. American beaver. 2. Beavers.] I. Title. II. Series.
QL737.R632M27 2000
599.37—dc21   99–18068

Manufactured in the United States of America
1 2 3 4 5 6 – JR – 05 04 03 02 01 00

This wet,
furry animal
is a beaver.

What is it
doing
with all of
these sticks?

This beaver is building a house.
A beaver house is called a *lodge*

A lodge is made of
tree branches and mud.

How do beavers build a lodge?

First, beavers cut down trees
with their long, sharp front teeth.

What color
are this
beaver's
teeth?

This beaver is standing up on
its back legs to chew a branch.

Its wide, flat
tail helps it
balance.

Next, beavers carry branches
and mud with their small front feet.

Beavers may build a lodge
in a stream, river, or small lake.

Sometimes beavers build a *dam* in the water.

Water cannot flow past a dam.

Water gets deeper on one side
of a dam, making a *beaver pond.*

Beavers build their lodge
in the pond.

Most of the lodge is above water.

How do beavers get inside?

The way into the lodge
is underwater.

Beavers are good swimmers.
Their back feet are *webbed*.

Animals with webbed feet
have skin joining their toes.

Webbed feet help beavers paddle in the water and swim quickly.

When it swims, a beaver
uses its tail to help it turn.

How else do beavers
use their tails?

Beavers use their tails
to stay safe from *predators*.

Predators are animals that
hunt and eat other animals.

If a swimming beaver sees
or smells a predator,

it lifts its tail up high. What do
you think the beaver will do next?

SLAP! The beaver hits
the water with its tail.

The loud noise tells other beavers
that a predator is near.

Beavers are not predators.
They are *herbivores.*

Herbivores are animals
that eat only plants.

These baby beavers are eating twigs and leaves.

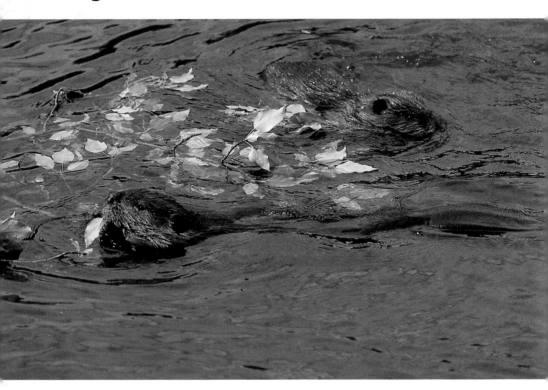

Babies drink milk from their mother when they are very young.

Baby beavers are called *kits.*

Kits can swim out of their lodge
when they are a week old.

Like all beavers, this kit can
keep its eyes open underwater.

Clear eyelids cover its eyes
when it swims.

This kit is tired of swimming.
It rides on its mother's tail.

This mother and kit are *grooming.*
Grooming keeps fur neat and clean.

Beavers comb their fur
with their back feet.

Beavers smooth their fur
with oil from their bodies.

This oil
makes their
fur water-
proof.

As a kit grows older,
it learns to fix leaks in a dam.

Soon the kit will be a super builder like its parents.

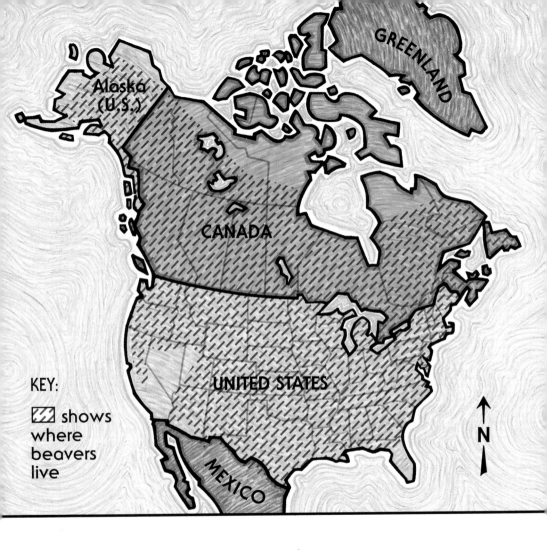

KEY:

☷ shows where beavers live

Find your state or province on this map.
Do beavers live near you?

Parts of a Beaver's Body

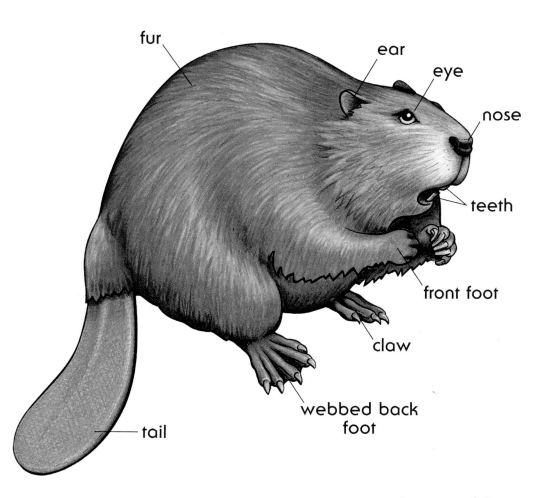

fur

ear

eye

nose

teeth

front foot

claw

webbed back foot

tail

Glossary

beaver pond: the deep water on one side of a beaver dam

dam: a wall built to hold back water. Beaver dams are made of sticks and mud.

grooming: keeping fur neat and clean

herbivores: animals that eat only plants

kits: baby beavers

lodge: a beaver house

predators: animals that hunt and eat other animals

webbed: having toes that are joined by skin

Hunt and Find

- beaver **dams** on pages 9–10, 26
- beavers **cutting down trees** on pages 6, 27
- beavers **grooming** on pages 24–25
- beaver **lodges** on pages 4–5, 8–9, 11
- a beaver **slapping** its tail on page 18
- kits **swimming** on pages 20–22

The publisher wishes to extend special thanks to our **series consultant,** Sharyn Fenwick. An elementary science-math specialist, Mrs. Fenwick was the recipient of the National Science Teachers Association 1991 Distinguished Teaching Award. In 1992, representing the state of Minnesota at the elementary level, she received the Presidential Award for Excellence in Math and Science Teaching.

Mike Dembeck

About the Author

Kathleen Martin-James was born in Toronto, Ontario. She lived in Sudbury, Ontario, until she was 14. Some of her happiest afternoons there were spent skating on the beaver pond near her house with her big brother, Jim. Since then, Kathleen has lived in many different places across Canada and the United States. She writes articles and takes photographs for magazines, newspapers, and newsletters. She loves to read and to write stories and poems. Kathleen lives in Wolfville, Nova Scotia, with her husband, Mike.

Photo Acknowledgments

The photographs in this book are reproduced through the courtesy of: © Milton H. Tierney, Jr./Visuals Unlimited, page 3; © Tom and Pat Leeson, pages 4, 6, 11, 17, 25, 27; © Gregory K. Scott, pages 5, 9; © Len Rue, Jr. pages 7, 8, 16, 19, 20, 26, 31, back cover; © Leonard Lee Rue III, pages 10, 12, 14, 18, 21, 22, 23, 24, front cover; © Leonard Lee Rue III/Visuals Unlimited, page 13; © Leonard Rue Enterprises/Visuals Unlimited, page 15.